LABRADOR RETRIEVER JOKE BOOK

WRITTEN BY
LABBY D. LAB

ISBN-13: 978-1978248939
ISBN-10: 1978248938

WHY DO BLACK LABS
RUN IN CIRCLES?

'CAUSE IT'S REALLY HARD
TO RUN IN SQUARES!

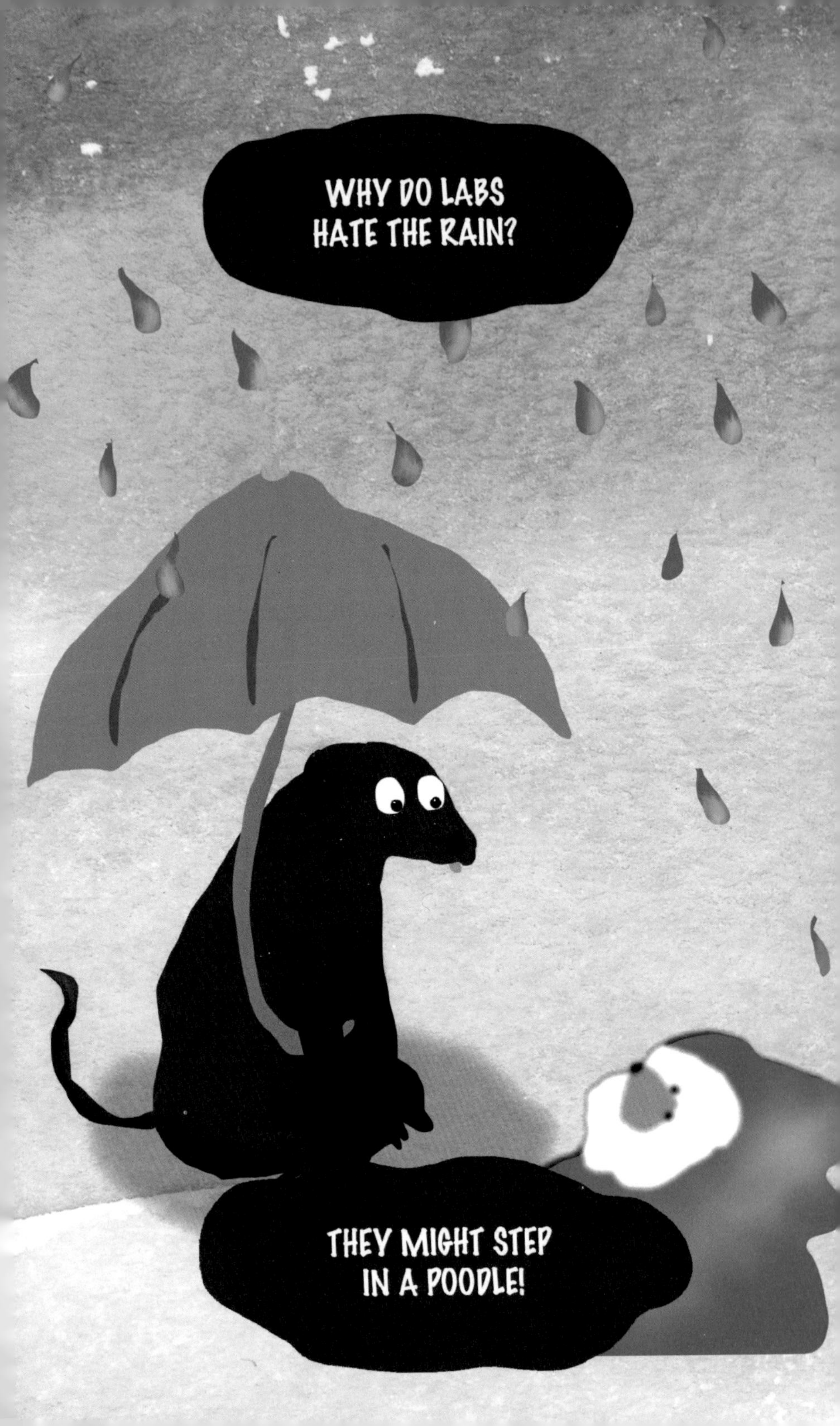
WHY DO LABS HATE THE RAIN?
THEY MIGHT STEP IN A POODLE!

WHAT DID THE BLACK LAB SAY TO THE GARDEN?
LETTUCE EAT!
A LAB BREEDER HAS 196 BLACK LABS IN HIS YARD
BUT WHEN HE ROUNDED THEM UP, HE HAD 200!

TWO OLD LABS
ARE IN THE LIBRARY.
ONE LEANS OVER
AND WHISPERS

"I JUST LET OUT
A LONG, SILENT FART!
WHAT SHOULD I DO?"

THE OTHER REPLIES,
"FIRST OFF, REPLACE THE
BATTERIES IN YOUR
HEARING AID"

WHY DO BLACK LAB
FARTS SMELL?

FOR THE BENEFIT OF PEOPLE
WHO ARE
HEARING IMPAIRED!

WHAT'S LARGE, GRAY, AND MAKES NO DIFFERENCE TO BLACK LABS?
NEVER MIND, IT'S IRRELEPHANT

A BLACK LAB, A KING CHARLES,
AND A POMERANIAN
WERE ALL LOST IN THE
DESERT WHEN THEY
FOUND A MAGIC LAMP!
A GENIE POPPED OUT AND
GRANTED THEM EACH ONE WISH.

THE POMERANIAN WISHED
SHE WAS BACK HOME.
POOF!
SHE WAS BACK HOME.

THE KING CHARLES WISHED
SHE WAS WITH HER FAMILY.
POOF,
SHE WAS BACK HOME
WITH HER FAMILY.

THE BLACK LAB SAID,
"AWWWWW, I WISH MY
FRIENDS WERE HERE"

WHY DO
LAB VAMPIRES
BELIEVE EVERYTHING
YOU TELL THEM?

BECAUSE
THEY'RE SUCKERS

WHAT DO YOU GET WHEN
YOU TRY TO CROSS A BLACK LAB
WITH A COMPUTER?

A LOT OF LITTLE BYTES.

WHAT'S A BLACK LABS
FAVORITE PIZZA?

PUPPERONI

WHAT KIND OF LABS
DONT LIKE PIZZA?

WEIR-DOUGHS!

WHAT'S THE
DIFFERENCE
BETWEEN A PIZZA
AND THESE
PIZZA LAB JOKES?

THESE LAB JOKES
CAN'T BE TOPPED!

OK, OK, ONE MORE
BLACK LAB PIZZA JOKE?

NAH, NEVER MIND,
IT'S TOO CHEESY!

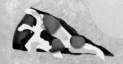

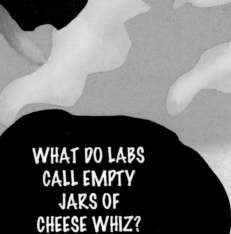

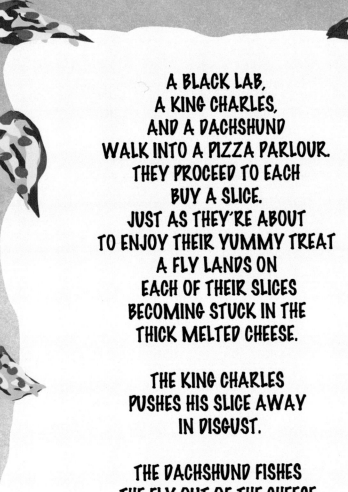

A BLACK LAB,
A KING CHARLES,
AND A DACHSHUND
WALK INTO A PIZZA PARLOUR.
THEY PROCEED TO EACH
BUY A SLICE.
JUST AS THEY'RE ABOUT
TO ENJOY THEIR YUMMY TREAT
A FLY LANDS ON
EACH OF THEIR SLICES
BECOMING STUCK IN THE
THICK MELTED CHEESE.

THE KING CHARLES
PUSHES HIS SLICE AWAY
IN DISGUST.

THE DACHSHUND FISHES
THE FLY OUT OF THE CHEESE
AND EATS IT,
SCHLURP!

THE LAB ALSO PICKS THE FLY
OUT OF HIS SLICE,
HOLDS IT OVER THE PLATE
AND STARTS YELLING
"SPIT IT OUT! SPIT IT OUT!"

THE BLACK LAB WAS
SO SHOCKED FROM SEEING
HIS FIRST SHIP WRECK

HE HAD TO
LET IT SINK IN

WHAT KIND OF
LAB MEDITATES
ON THE FULL MOON?

AWARE-WOLF!

A LAB OWNER
COMES HOME FROM
THE INTERNATIONAL MARKET

"HERE BOY!
YOU WANT
SOME BRAZILIAN TREATS?"

THE LAB REPLIES

"OH MY GOSH!
I'M SO LUCKY!!!
WAIT...
HOW MANY IS A
BRAZILIAN?"

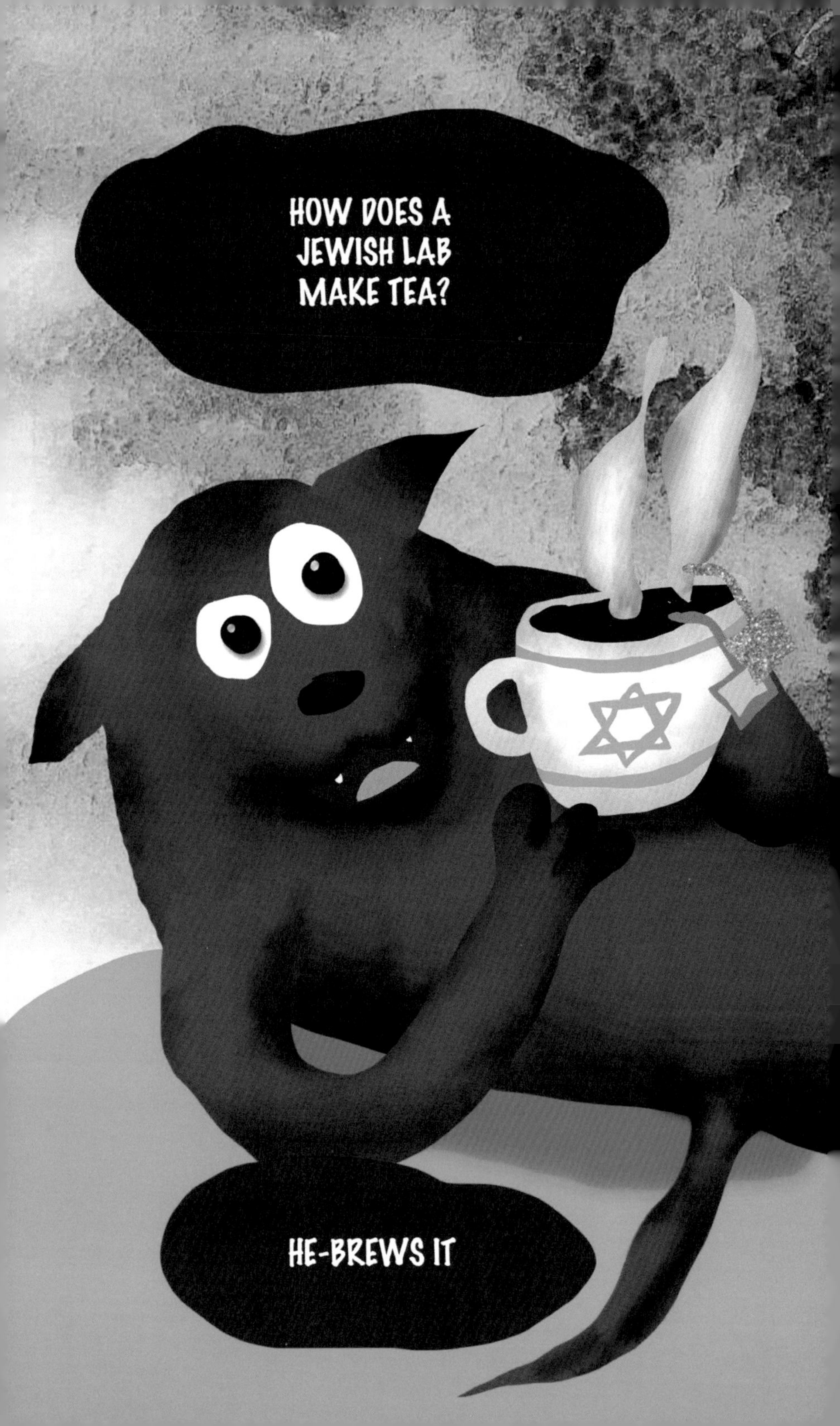
HOW DOES A JEWISH LAB MAKE TEA?
HE-BREWS IT

WHAT DID THE
LAB SAY
AFTER EATING
AT THE DALMATIAN
RESTAURANT?

THAT REALLY HIT THE SPOT!

THAT BLACK LAB
IS A REALLY
MEAN COOK!

HE WHIPS
THE CREAM
AND
BEATS THE EGGS

HOW CAN YOU
TELL IF A LAB
IS A GOOD COOK?

HE MAKES GREAT
USE OF HIS THYME!

A MAN WENT
TO VISIT A FRIEND
AND WAS
AMAZED TO FIND
HIM PLAYING CHESS
WITH HIS BLACK LAB.

HE WATCHED THE GAME
IN ASTONISHMENT
FOR A WHILE.

"I CAN HARDLY BELIEVE MY EYES!"
HE EXCLAIMED.
"THAT LABS
THE SMARTEST DOG
I'VE EVER SEEN."

"NAH,
HE'S NOT
SO SMART,"
THE FRIEND REPLIED.

"I'VE BEATEN HIM
THREE GAMES
OUT OF FIVE."

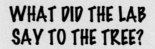

WHILE AT A
DOGGY DINNER PARTY
A BLACK LAB FARTS.

THE
KING CHARLES SAYS
"HOW DARE YOU
FART IN FRONT OF ME!"

THE LAB REPLIES
"I'M SORRY,
I DIDN'T REALIZE
IT WAS YOUR TURN"

MY LAB IS DEPRESSED

HOW DO YOU KNOW?

EVERY TIME
I ASK HOW HIS LIFE'S GOING,
ALL HE SAYS IS
"RUFF!"

SOMEONE STOLE
MY BLACK LAB
MOOD RING!

I HAVE NO IDEA
HOW I FEEL
ABOUT IT!

KNOCK KNOCK
WHOSE THERE

DOORBELL
REPAIR LAB!

HOW DO BLACK LAB
ASTRONAUGHTS
ORGANIZE
SPACE PARTIES?

THEY PLANET!

WHY DID THE LAB
ROLL TOILET PAPER
DOWN THE HILL

SO IT COULD
GET TO THE BOTTOM

WHERE DID THE LAB GO
WHEN HIS
TAIL FELL OFF?

THE RETAIL STORE!

WHAT HAPPENS
WHEN THE BLACK LAB
ATE A CLOVE OF GARLIC?

HIS BARK
WAS WORSE THAN HIS BITE!

WHATS A BLACK LABS
FAVORITE COMEDIAN?

GROWL-CHO MARX

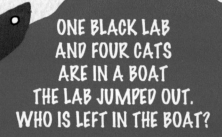

ONE BLACK LAB
AND FOUR CATS
ARE IN A BOAT
THE LAB JUMPED OUT.
WHO IS LEFT IN THE BOAT?

NOBODY,
THEY WERE ALL
COPYCATS!

WHAT HAPPENED
WHEN THE CAT WON
THE BLACK LAB
BEAUTY CONTEST?

IT WAS A
CAT-HAS-TROPHY

WHAT DID
THE WINNER SAY?

CHECK
MEEEE-OUWT!

WHAT DO YOU GET
WHEN YOU CROSS A BLACK LAB
AND A HYENA?

I DON'T KNOW,
BUT IF IT LAUGHS, GIVE HIM A TREAT.

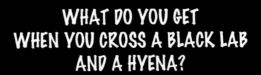

WHATS THE DIFFERENCE BETWEEN
A BLACK LAB AND A MARINE BIOLOGIST?

ONE WAGS A TALE,
THE OTHER
TAGS A WHALE!

WHATS THE DIFFERENCE
BETWEEN MY LAB AND A PIZZA?

(DON'T KNOW)

IN THAT CASE, I'LL BE
ORDERING DINNER TONIGHT!

A BLACK LAB AT A
BASEBALL GAME KEPT WONDERING
WHY THE BALL WAS GETTING
BIGGER
AND BIGGER.

THEN IT HIT HIM!

WHAT DO YOU MEAN,
MY LAB CHASED A GUY ON A BIKE?

MY LAB DOESN'T EVEN OWN A BIKE!

DID YOU HEAR
ABOUT THE BLACK LAB
WHO HAD NO NOSE?

I HEARD HE SMELLED
AWFUL!

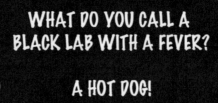

WHAT DO YOU CALL A
BLACK LAB WITH A FEVER?

A HOT DOG!

WHAT ABOUT A COLD LAB?

A PUPSICLE

AND IF THAT LAB
GETS EVEN COLDER?

THAT'S A CHILI DOG!

WAIT! THAT COLD
LAB IS SITTING ON A RABBIT!

OH, THAT'S
A CHILI DOG ON A BUN!

WHAT DO MY BLACK LAB
AND MY PHONE HAVE IN COMMON?

THEY BOTH
HAVE COLLAR ID

THE LAB TOLD HIS GIRLFRIEND
SHE DREW HER EYEBROWS
WAY TOO HIGH

SHE LOOKED VERY SURPRISED!

WHAT HAPPENED
WHEN THE BLACK LAB WENT
TO A FLEA CIRCUS?

HE STOLE THE SHOW

WHERE DO LABS HATE TO SHOP?

THE FLEA MARKET!

DID YOU HEAR
ABOUT THE SPECIAL AT
THE PET STORE?

BUY 1 DOG
GET ONE FLEA!

A BLACK LAB
WALKS INTO A BAR
ORDERS A DRINK
WHEN SUDDENLY HE HEARS
SOMEONE SHOUT "HEY CUTIE!"
THE LAB LOOKS AROUND BUT
NO ONE IS THERE
"HEY! NICE BLACK TAIL!"
THE LAB LOOKS UP AGAIN
BUT NOBODY IS THERE.
"HEY! CUTE SHINY NOSE!"
THE LAB FRUSTRATED
CALLS OVER THE BARTENDER ASKING
"HEY, YOU TALKIN TO ME?"
THE BARTENDER REPLIES
"IT'S NOT ME!
IT'S THE COMPLMENTARY PEANUTS!"

A
THREE LEGGED LAB
WALKS INTO A BAR
AND SAYS
"I'M LOOKING FOR THE MAN
WHO SHOT MY PAW"

WOULD YOU RATHER A
BLACK LAB CHASE YOU OR A LION?

I'D RATHER
HE CHASE THE LION!

WHAT DO YOU DO
WHEN YOU SEE YOUR LAB
EATING A DICTIONARY?

TAKE THE WORDS
RIGHT OUT OF HIS MOUTH!

A LAB IS ON A BEACH
WATCHING A HIPPIE
DROWN IN THE WATER!

THE LIFEGUARD SAYS
"AREN'T YOU GONNA
DO SOMETHING?"

THE LAB REPLIES
"NO WAY,
HE'S TOO FAR OUT"

A LAB THINKS:
"WOW,
HUMANS BRING ME FOOD EVERY DAY,
THEY HAVE ME LIVE
IN A AWESOME HOUSE,
ITS NOT COLD, NO RAIN,
THEY TAKE CARE OF ME...
HUMANS MUST BE GODS..."

A CAT THINKS:
"WOW, HUMANS BRING ME FOOD EVERY DAY,
THEY HAVE ME LIVE IN A AWESOME HOUSE, I
TS NOT COLD, NO RAIN,
THEY TAKE CARE OF ME...
I MUST BE GOD!"

ABOUT THE AUTHOR

LAB JOKES WAS WRITTEN
BY LABBY D. LAB

LABBY IS A FUN LOVIN' LAB
FROM WISCONSIN
HE LOVES TREATS,
SNUGGLES, PIZZA,
TELLING JOKES
AND WRITING BOOKS!

19668907R00027

Made in the USA
Middletown, DE
06 December 2018